Preface

In the early 1980s I heard that a customer always buys the benefit of a product. That made me interested, and I wanted to learn what a customer benefits is. With this knowledge I could probably improve my skills as a salesman and achieve better results. But there was also another interesting question that this matter raised. How many benefits are there? Thousands, hundreds, tens, or less? I started to look for the answers in the literature. After looking through numerous marketing books and articles, I recognized that customer benefit is one of the main concepts. Nevertheless, I could not find a satisfactory description of customer benefits, or an answer to the number of customer benefits.

This was the starting point for my study. And I'm happy to share the results of my work with you now. I have considered both the B2C and B2B environment in the results. Consumers and companies experience the same benefits, but there can be a difference in the sources of the benefits, and there can also be different emphasis of the benefits. In B2B selling you need to take a note of all the various needs of the actors in the supply chain besides the needs of the end customer.

I have developed a model in which the concept of 'customer benefit' is clearly defined, and all the potential customer benefits are listed and grouped. The four level model (source, rational, emotional, and core level) gives understanding of the numerous processes (based on material sources, sources in logistics, and social sources) that can lead to a customer benefit. It allows easy identification of any customer benefit both in the B2B and the B2C environment. Simultaneously, it is possible to recognize lacking or weak customer benefits, which enables planning and implementing of improvements in a product, a service, or in an operation. The model also provides an excellent platform for developing customer-oriented activities, and evident arguments of any products and service products. Furthermore, the model always gives the salesman or the marketer the means of answering one of the most essential question from their customer, "What's there in it for me?"

This book is beneficial for all who are looking for better results through customer-oriented communication, argumentation and operation.

Robert Henriksson
Helsinki

Kustantaja: BoD – Books on Demand, Helsinki, Suomi
Valmistaja: BoD – Books on Demand, Norderstedt, Saksa
ISBN: 978-952-286-623-3

Index

1 Introduction: Benefit – a self-evident or an elusive concept? 2
We satisfy our needs and wants with benefits 2
Why is so important to understand what a benefit is? 3
How has our understanding of benefits evolved? 4
2 Values and benefits 8
Terminal values and instrumental values 8
The terminal values are benefits 10
Grouping benefits 15
Core benefits 16
3 The materialistic sources of benefits 18
The features of tangible and intangible products 18
The advantages of a product 19
4 The sources of benefits in logistics 20
The flows in logistics 21
The advantages in logistics 21
5 The social sources of benefits 21
Customer service 22
Instrumental values 22
6 The model for identifying customer benefits 27
The structure of the model 27
The model for identifying customer benefits 30
7 Theses and definitions 31
Five theses of customer benefits 31
Benefits and added value 32
Benefits and a brand 32
8 Communicating benefits 33
Market 33
Benefits and positioning 35
Benefits and advertising 36
Benefits and selling 37
Product benefits and their processes 39
The benefits of a Kickbike 39
Building the processes 40
The benefits and their processes in logistics 43
Social benefits and their processes 45
To remember 47
References 48

1 Introduction: Benefit – a self-evident or an elusive concept?

We all know what a benefit is. Or do we? When reflecting more deeply this main concept in marketing and selling, you may recognize bit by bit that it is not so easy to define this concept. Not to mention making a complete list of all the benefits.

We satisfy our needs and wants with benefits

Hey, let's go shopping!
Why?
We could find something nice that we don't yet know that we need!
But I can already manage with everything that I have.
Don't be boring!

We live in abundance. When we set the benchmark for our very survival, the market is full of products and services, without which we could survive quite well. Our standard of living allows us to satisfy all kinds of needs and wants. From the above dialogue, we can see that our struggle to satisfy our needs has both a bio-physiological and a psychological-sociological dimension. In general, the biological-physiological dimension is seen as needs and the psycho-sociological dimension as wants. In other words, people eat to live and live to eat at the same time.

I guess that having wants is necessary, as well as characteristic of human nature. Drawing a line between the needs and wants is quite problematic. For example, only flavouring food could be interpreted as satisfying a want. We cannot escape our wants, for example, by becoming a hermit somewhere in the wilderness, because even this choice can be interpreted as a desire to satisfy a want. In addition, all the needs and wants can form a multi-threaded tangle in which a separation can become impossible. Our interpretation is affected by our subjective values, of course, which can also change according to our life situation. Therefore, it can be difficult to find a definition for the needs and wants, which would be completely satisfactory. In my opinion, it is not always necessary at all. But whether the question is about a need or a want, we will not acquire a product or service if it does not provide us a benefit. Although we may not always be clearly aware of the benefits that a product or service offers us.

In many ways we are creatures of our habits, and hence not always aware of the reasons for our decisions. When looking at the purchasing decisions we do without considering the benefits, these products and services belong to the so-called *Low-*

Involvement category. For example, many groceries belong to this category. When buying these products, we do not sacrifice time or effort to make our choices. Our choices are largely based on our experience and our customs. In other words, we are constantly repeating things that we have learned in the past to be beneficial.

Similarly, we are considering more our purchasing decisions when the acquisition is more valuable, or when it involves various uncertainties and risks, or where our previous experience of the product is poor. That is, when procurements include the possibility of some level of remorse. These types of procurements belong to the so-called *High-Involvement* category. These include, for example, a number of consumer durables and investments, of course. We are aware then more clearly of the benefits of the product or service.

It is equally difficult to draw a line between *Low-Involvement* and *High-Involvement products*. The difference is again often subjective and can change according to the situation. All products and services, however, always provide benefits regardless of the category they belong to.

Why is so important to understand what a benefit is?

In his book *The Fundamentals of Selling*, Charles Futrell[1] gives the following three reasons why understanding of benefits is important.

1. The customer buys always the benefits – not the features or the advantages.
2. By presenting the benefits the customer understands better how the product satisfies his or her needs.
3. By presenting the benefits you can improve your sales.

If the customer really always buys the benefit of a product or service, then having an understanding of what the benefits are and applying this knowledge, we can always be customer-oriented. This can provide a competitive advantage and enable us to achieve better results, regardless of what we sell. But what everything of the customer benefits should we know?

Of course, it would be important to know what is meant by a benefit. But at the same time the benefits wake up an interesting question - how many benefits are there? Are there thousands, hundreds, tens, or less? If the number of benefits prove to be few, they could certainly all be named and, perhaps, set into groups. Then it would be easy to find out what the benefits of the various products and services provide customers, but at the same time it would be possible to say what the

[1] Charles M. Futrell, American professor in marketing, http://futrell-www.tamu.edu

benefits are missing. This information would be helpful in creating marketing communications and developing sales skills, but also in product development.

If we are able to present to our clients the benefits, they are more likely to buy the product. But how do we make sure that our customers are buying the product from us and not from the neighbouring store that sells the same products? In other words, it is not enough that we are able to present the benefits of the product, but at the same time, we must also be able to present the benefits that make the potential customers buy from us.

Understanding the benefits could also give a better perspective to understand what customer-orientation means and how it differs from product-orientation. Similarly, we could get a better understanding of what added-value means and find a new perspective upon a brand.

How has our understanding of benefits evolved?

The benefit is a very common concept in all walks of life. We are constantly thinking about what benefits different things could provide us. However, there seems to be quite a few definitions of a benefit, not to mention good definitions. Apparently, our understanding of what is meant with a benefit, has been considered and is still considered as so self-evident, that there has not been a need for a good definition. The general perception is that a benefit is something that has a rewarding effect to us. The word benefit has a number of synonyms. The most common of these is an advantage. Other synonyms are income, value, utility, and profit.

Customer benefits are quite frequently handled in marketing and sales literature. In the 1970s, models were presented in which the benefit is seen as a result of the process. The processes leading to the benefits derive from product features. In 1970, Shirley Young and Barbara Feigin presented the *Grey Benefit Chain* model, developed by Hal Lee, in which features lead to functional, practical and emotional benefits. In 1972, Paul E. Green, Yoram Wind and Arun K. Jain presented the *Benefit Bundle Analysis* model, which can be used to find out all the benefits a product can provide. In 1976, James H. Myers presented the *Benefit Structure Analysis (BSA)*, a model that has been prepared for product development.

Although the customer benefit is the central concept in the above-mentioned models, a definition is not given in any of the models. Regarding our understanding of customer benefits, the best part in these models is the idea that the benefits are a result of a process. A benefit does not arise spontaneously, there is always a source, and the source is located in the product features.

In 1982, Jonathan Gutman issued the Means-End Chain Model. The purpose of his model is to find out the link between the product features and our terminal values. Laddering technique is used to clarify the terminal values. By placing the question, *"Why is this so important to you?"* it is possible to uncover the underlying motives of the interviewee's choice. Thus, when studying the connection, Gutman extends the processes from the materialistic world into sociology. This is probably the first model, which sets out a clear definition of customer benefits – *"Benefits are the desirable consequences of attributes"*. This definition follows the traditional perception of the benefits and strengthens the hypotheses why definitions of benefits are rare.

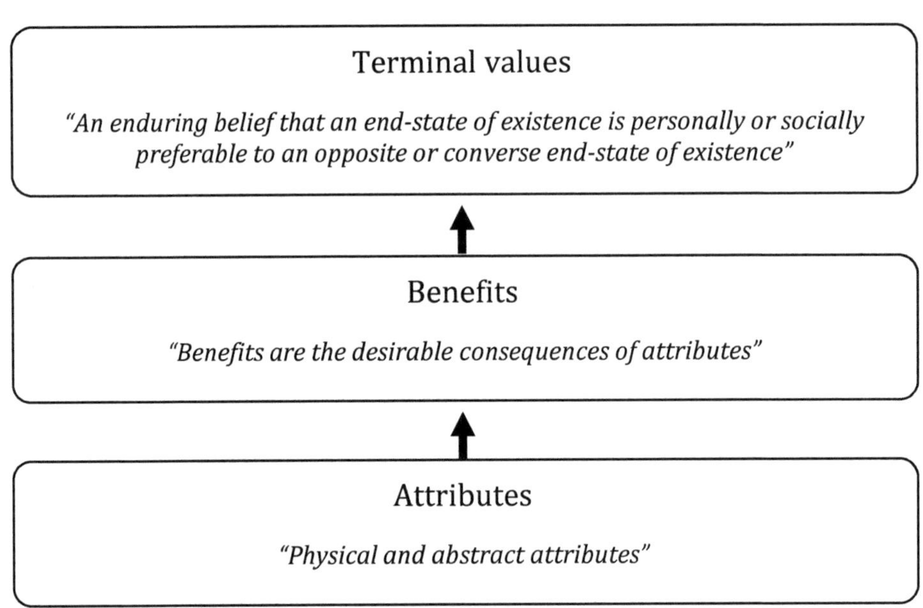

In the Means-End Chain model, the process is studied starting from the attributes towards the terminal values utilizing the laddering technique.

The customer benefits are also used for segmentation. Russell Haley, who studied and developed in the 1960s customer segments, considers in 1983 the psychographic customer segments to be problematic. He noted that it is difficult to make any segmentation based upon sensory benefits, emotional benefits, and affiliative benefits. He recognizes that these cannot be measured. But Haley, like most of the other researchers, does not provide a definition of a benefit. I presume that he also sees the benefits as something that has a positive effect.

In 1984, the American marketing professor Charles Futrell published his book *The Fundamentals of Selling*, which has since appeared in several editions, the last one is dated 2006. Futrell presents in this book the FAB model (Features, Advantages, Benefits). It differs in an interesting way from all of the previous models. The concepts of benefit and advantage are defined as two different matters. The three-phase model starts from the features of the product. In the next phase are the advantages of the product and in the third phase the benefits of the product. Furthermore, the model is also used in the opposite direction for proving the identified benefits. Futrell's definition of a benefit is slightly more detailed than any of the previous definitions: *"A product benefit is a favourable result the buyer receives from the product because of a particular advantage that has the ability to satisfy a buyer's need".*

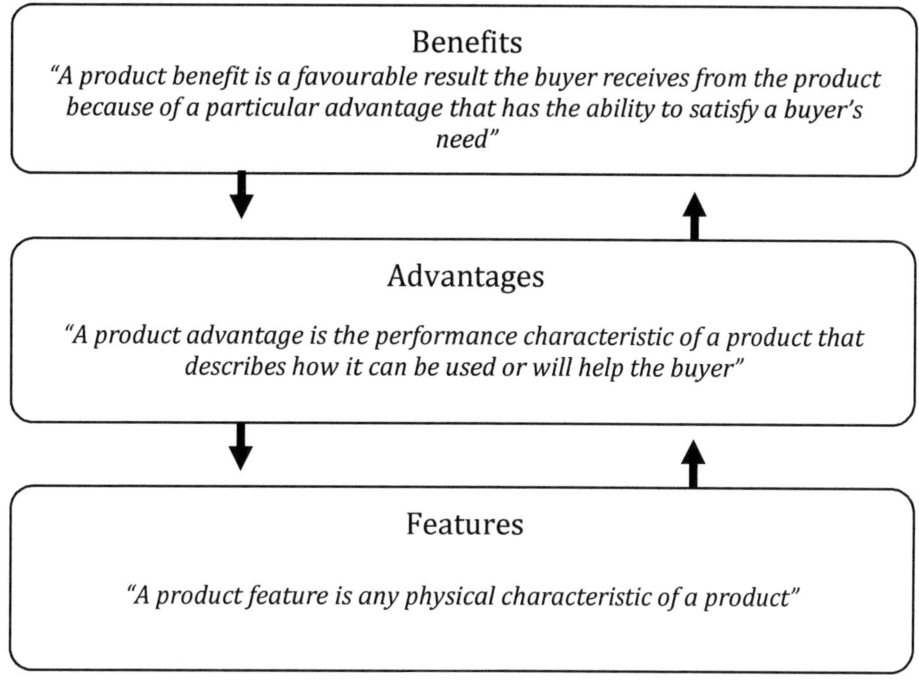

In the FAB model, advantages and benefits are defined as two different concepts. The model is used in both directions, for deriving the benefits, and for proving the identified benefits.

Marketing literature shows the concept of the core benefits. By definition, a product or service contains a key benefit which makes the consumer buy the product. Two synonymous expressions are used in the literature, Core Benefit and Core Product. The following is AMA's (American Marketing Association) definition of the Core Benefit.

AMA's definition of Core Benefit

The main benefit why a customer buys the product. The core benefit varies from buyer to buyer. The core benefit can derive either from the tangible product or customer service, or the augmented product.

I think the customers' purchasing decisions are often affected by many factors at the same time. That's why I settle a little critical of the core benefit. I will return to the core benefit later, when I present a completely different definition.

In summary, we can state a benefit is the ultimate reason why we buy products and services. Perceptions of the benefits can be generally stated in our everyday life as everything that has a positive effect upon us. In academic sources, the benefits can be seen more analytically as a result of processes, which have their source in the product features. But, the definitions and examples presented in the literature do not reveal clearly what benefits are, or provide an answer to the interesting question how many benefits there are.

2 Values and benefits

A basic knowledge about human values is essential in order to understand the customer benefits. As a starting point it can be noted that the values that we have adopted direct our behaviour as do our objectives. We will soon learn how values are connected to customer benefits. Rokeach[2] (1973) defines value as follows:

The definition of values

An enduring belief that a mode of conduct and an end-state of existence is personally or socially preferable to an opposite or converse mode of conduct and an end-state of existence.

According to Rokeach, all humans have values that continuously direct our choices. However, there is not only one value that directs our behaviour, but all the values that we have adopted, which form a so-called value system. Everyone has his or her own value system. The value system is not completely static; it can change according to experiences and life situations.

Terminal values and instrumental values

Our values can be divided into two categories, the terminal values and the instrumental values. Terminal values are the end-state of existence. They can be personal or social. In both cases, the terminal values are positive feelings that we would like to experience. We can achieve the terminal values by following the instrumental values, that is, by behaving in a way that also other people feel that a is a good way of conduct. In other words, the terminal values are the rewards of exercising the instrumental values, and a terminal value manifests itself as a positive feeling.

[2] Milton Rokeach (1918–1988), a Polish-American social psychologist.

Rokeach (1973) presents 18 terminal values and 18 instrumental values.

Terminal values – 'end-state of existence'
A comfortable life (a prosperous life)
An exciting life (a stimulated, active life)
A sense of accomplishment (lasting contribution)
Wisdom (a mature understanding of life)
Inner harmony (freedom from inner conflict)
Equality (brotherhood, equal opportunity for all)
Happiness (contentedness)
Freedom (independence, free choice)
Pleasure (an enjoyable, leisurely life)
A world of beauty (beauty of nature and the arts)
A world at peace (free of war and conflict)
National security (protection from attack)
Family security (taking care of loved ones)
Self-respect (self-esteem)
Social recognition (respect, admiration)
Salvation (saved, eternal life)
True friendship (close companionship)
Mature love (sexual and spiritual intimacy)

Instrumental values – 'mode of conduct'
Ambitious (hard-working, aspiring)
Open-minded (accepting, broad-minded)
Capable (competent, effective)
Cheerful (light-hearted, joyful)
Clean (neat, tidy)
Courageous (standing up for your beliefs)
Forgiving (willing to pardon others)
Helpful (working for the welfare of others)
Honest (sincere, truthful)
Imaginative (daring, creative)
Independent (self-reliant, self-sufficient)
Intellectual (intelligent, reflective)
Logical (consistent, rational)
Loving (affectionate, tender)
Obedient (dutiful, respectful)
Polite courteous and well-mannered
Responsible (dependable, reliable)
Self-controlled (restrained, self-disciplined)

Instrumental values can be divided into two categories - moral values and knowledge values. The difference between these can be recognized in an interesting way. If we do not comply with a moral value, we can get it as a result of a bad conscience. When we experience a sense of shame, it is due to a lack of a knowledge value. If we do not feel bad conscience or shame when we should, apparently the relevant instrumental value does not exist in our value system.

The terminal values are benefits

As I stated earlier, the terminal values are positive feelings that we would like to experience. We can achieve these feelings by exercising the instrumental values, that is, by behaving in a way that others perceive also a good way to behave.

But we can gain the same positive feelings in other ways than through good behaviour – by buying and consuming. All plant and equipment, on which we spend our money, evoke positive emotions in us. Already the buying process itself can generate positive emotions. So, we can achieve the terminal values, through a material and a social mode of conduct. The difference between these two options is described in an old wisdom. Good behaviour does not cost you anything, but consumption requires always resources.

I suggest that the terminal values are benefits. This is the main statement in my study. I interpret that the terminal values, that is, the benefits are always positive emotions. I would also like to make a few additional interpretations.

1. The terminal values can be divided into two groups according to the order they emerge. The prior group consists of the terminal values that we will achieve first. Without achieving these, we are not able to achieve the latter group. The prior group includes the benefits and the latter group of the core benefits, that is, the feelings of inner harmony, satisfaction and happiness.
2. Since the context is commercial, I exclude three terminal values. With money, we do not get salvation, a true friendship, or love. Sure, these have been traded, and will be traded in the future, but as products or services they lack the sense of authenticity. In addition, marketing of these include unethical or even illegal things. On the other hand, salvation, true friendship and love are often essential to gain the core benefits.
3. I suggest that the feeling of joy, which is defined by Rokeach as an instrumental value, is also a terminal value. That is, the feeling of joy is both an instrumental value and a terminal value. By being joyful we can make other joyful too. Joy is said to be contagious.
4. Rokeach has distinguished three dimensions of a sense of safety, world peace, national security, and the safety of the family. The feeling of safety is the common denominator for all three. Thus, all of these can be combined to the feeling of safety.

5. Self-esteem is included in two terminal values; in self-respect and social acceptance. The first is about self-esteem as an internal issue, and the other is about self-esteem as an external issue. I combine these two into self-esteem, which is a feeling about our self.
6. Beautiful World (the beautiful nature and art) refers to many things which we can enjoy through our senses. That's why I suggest a wider focus of the subject and retitle it as feeling of pleasure.

Based upon the interpretations, we end up with the following three core benefits, and ten customer benefits. As well as the three terminal values, which are not suitable in a commercial context, I've have also added into the table my interpretation about the personal and social dimension of each value.

Core benefits	**Dimension**
Feeling of satisfaction	Personal
Feeling of inner harmony	Personal
Feeling of happiness	Personal
Customer benefits	**Dimension**
Feeling of wisdom	Personal
Feeling of comfort	Personal
Feeling of accomplishment	Personal
Feeling of safety	Personal/social
Feeling of equality	Social
Feeling of thrill	Personal
Feeling of pleasure	Personal
Feeling of freedom	Personal
Feeling of joy	Personal
Self-esteem	Personal/social
Non-commercial terminal values	**Dimension**
Feeling of love	Personal/social
Feeling of salvation	Personal
Feeling of true friendship	Personal/social

I will describe the benefits in detail below and return to the core benefits a little later.

Feeling of wisdom

Our mind is filled with a feeling of wisdom, when we reach our goals without wasting resources. Similarly, we feel bad about our decisions that turn out to be unpremeditated, or even stupid. The consumer's remorse is aptly called the *"buyer's hangover"*. Many companies refer to our sense of wisdom. For example, Anttila's advertising states *"wise money buys from Anttila – be smart, come to Anttila."* The Gigantti chain, in turn, says: *"it just is stupid to pay too much."* Similar petitions to the customer's sense of wisdom can be found in many other ads. But we are wasting our money also if we purchase a product with a service life, or whose maintenance costs are not in line with our expectations. In other words, the product's durability and low operating costs are also related to a sense of wisdom. It is said that the poor cannot afford to buy bad. More expensive but more durable, or a product with lower maintenance costs can be the most profitable option. That is, the lowest priced option will not always be the wisest thing to do.

Feeling of comfort

A feeling of comfort is associated with three dimensions. First of all, we can experience a feeling of comfort when something is easy to carry out, or someone else helps us. Also, when performing it can be done quickly. For example, the product must be easy to acquire. *"Make it easy for your customer"* is a familiar precept in marketing and sales work. Also, *"to go the extra mile"* is certainly familiar for many sales people. Second, we can experience a feeling of comfort when something is ergonomically just right. Or when the installation, adjustment and use of a product are easy and quick. The feeling of comfort is linked to many products, but they are equally important in services. When we are sitting in a comfortable chair, we will be happy with the barber, hairdresser, in a vehicle, at a restaurant, etc. Third, when we get hungry, thirsty, when it is too cold or hot, when we become sick or ill, or when we receive any other inconvenient stimulus, we lose the feelings of comfort. Through our actions and choices, we can restore the feeling of comfort, and we can through our knowledge and experience also prevent the inconvenience from occurring.

Feeling of accomplishment

When we have fulfilled a task, for example, have completed a repair work, we gain a feeling of accomplishment. The harder we have had to struggle for our goal, the stronger the feeling of accomplishment tends to be. Feeling of accomplishment gives mental strength, and is thus an important source of motivation. The opposite feelings are frustration and inadequacy, which have a demotivating effect, respectively. As sales people, we can help our customers achieve a feeling of accomplishment. Again, this is associated with the previously mentioned familiar guideline – *"make it easy for your customer"*. Our customers can experience an acquisition to be very difficult and demanding measure. By implementing the guidelines, we can get our customers to experience a feeling of accomplishment. And even better, it would be great if we would be able to awaken a feeling of accomplishment that would exceed our customers' expectations.

Feeling of safety

Feeling of safety has a personal and a social dimension. In the personal dimension, we make choices for our safety. In the social dimension, we take into account other people, and make choices where safety extends to loved ones, neighbours, etc. A feeling of fear is the opposite of a feeling of safety. It is not uncommon that by engendering the feeling of fear, marketers try to establish a purchase decision. For example, an insurance, medications and nutrition supplements are products that provide a feeling of safety. But security is linked with innumerable other products - safety is a selling point, which is invoked very often. Products can be tested - or produced in a particular way so that we can count on them to be safe. Safety is such a major factor, that directives and laws have been launched to provide a control of products and their manufacturing.

Feeling of equality

As a customer, we want to sense a feeling of equality in relation to other customers. In other words, a feeling of equality is related to our concept of justice. We do not allow queue-jumps, and we do not accept that the seller depreciates our want to buy or our purchase edge. Our customers want to be able to enjoy the same products and services as any other customer. Children often want to get the same products as their good friends to feel equal in the group. Hence, it is common to hear the appeal from children, *"the other guys have it – why cannot I get one?"* In addition, feeling of equality seems to be related to the need of strengthening a child's self-esteem. And that is not just confined to children. A similar need exists in adults.

Feeling of thrill

Uncertainty about the future creates a feeling of excitement. We can experience the feeling of excitement as a very meaningful and an up-lifting experience when the tension does not interfere too much with our need of safety. And when it does not involve other negative or unpleasant factors. For example, books, movies, games and competitions are products that can offer us a feeling of thrill. Follow-up stories competently take advantage of our need for excitement – a story is always cut at an exciting situation. In games and competitions, the chance factors increase a feeling of thrill.

Feeling of pleasure

We can sense a feeling of pleasure through our five senses. With our sense of sight, we can enjoy many beautiful things. With our hearing, for example, we can enjoy music. With a sense of touch we can enjoy the feel warmth and a contact. The sense of smell and taste allow us to enjoy the aroma and good taste of food. With our senses, we can enjoy a multitude of products and services. Also, the products that are originally developed for other purposes than stimulating a feeling of pleasure. For example, we purchase a car to be able to travel quickly and conveniently from place to place. In fact, the most important criterion in choosing a car may be the colour, design or leather upholstery fragrance that evokes feelings of pleasure.

Feeling of freedom

A feeling of freedom does not only include the physical freedom, but also a mental freedom. We can experience a feeling of freedom in many areas and in many ways. Freedom is the opportunity to choose and decide independently on important issues without experiencing guilt, pressure or threat. The feeling of freedom is to be able to break free from the monotony of everyday life, or a variety of duties. We recognize the value of freedom, when deprived of our freedom, or when we are not able for some other reason to experience it. For example, tourism provides us with an opportunity to experience the feeling of freedom. In addition, we achieve the feeling of freedom by purchasing a car or any other vehicle that will allow us moving about more freely.

Feeling of joy

A feeling of joy is associated with a smile, a laugh, and rejoices. The often heard phrase *"laughter makes life longer"* tells us how much we appreciate the feeling of joy. But the feeling of joy may not always have to be visible. The feeling of joy is the opposite of the feeling of sadness. It is probably safe to suggest that the occasional feeling of sadness is necessary to experience moments of joy. For example, a stand-up comedian represents a product which is intended to evoke the feeling of joy. But many other products offer the opportunity to experience the feeling of joy, such as comedies (theatre, films), books, and games. In addition, the interaction with cheerful people can make us cheerful too.

Self-esteem

Self-esteem is a feeling of our social appreciation, that is, our understanding of our position in a group and the esteem we receive from others. Feeling our social appreciation is often relative, that is, our self-esteem can be affected by the dignity received by the others in the group. Jealousy can then be seen as a manifestation of a low self-esteem. A strong self-esteem may be more difficult to recognize than low self-esteem. A person with a strong self-esteem does not have the need to express things in a way that are characteristic of a person who has a low self-esteem. A weak self-esteem has many manifestations. These include envy, very often a need to awaken and get attention one way or another. But low self-esteem may also occur in just an opposite way.

The challenge of identifying emotions

Emotions are associated with a variety of interesting dimensions. First of all, emotions are not permanent. In particular, the emotions that we achieve by buying products and services. They can be very short-lived. Second, it may be difficult to detect a clear distinction between different emotions, because we can experience several different emotions at the same time. In addition, feelings can be in a reciprocal relationship. A feeling of freedom can give rise to a feeling of joy. A strong feeling of pleasure can also give rise to a feeling of joy, etc. Third, emotions are subjective, and therefore, they are very difficult to measure and compare. For example, how can we know that we are happier than another happy person, or experience a greater feeling of freedom than anyone else? On the other hand, it is easier to detect a missing positive feeling, that is, a lack of a benefit. And all these emotions, that is, the benefits are just the very things that our customers want to experience. In other words, our customers are buying a product's benefits, as Futrell has stated.

Grouping benefits

In the literature, benefits are divided into many different groups. In my opinion, these are not all suitable for the proper grouping of benefits. A good grouping should be all-inclusive, but at the same time the groups must be at an appropriate and a consistent conceptual level. In addition, the groups should help us in understanding the background of emotions. The following four groups meet these requirements.

Economic benefit

An economic benefit refers always to how we use our resources, that is, issues such as the price, terms of payment, financing, operation costs, durability, residual value, and income.

Functional benefits

Benefits associated with external factors needed to be fulfilled or with solving a problem, are functional benefits. Also, the basic physiological needs, which are essential for the maintenance of life, belong to this group.

Experiential benefits

The benefits that are transmitted through our senses are experiential benefits. This group also includes cognitive stimuli such as a sense of variation; a feeling of tension, emotions awaken by imagination, and mind-refreshing reflections.

Symbolic benefit

Self-esteem is the only benefit in this group.

According to the previous definitions, we end up with the next grouping.

Customer benefit	Dimension	Group
Feeling of wisdom	Personal	Economic benefit
Feeling of comfort	Personal	Functional benefit
Feeling of accomplishment	Personal	Functional benefit
Feeling of safety	Personal/social	Functional benefit
Feeling of equality	Social	Functional benefit
Feeling of thrill	Personal	Experiential benefit
Feeling of pleasure	Personal	Experiential benefit
Feeling of freedom	Personal	Experiential benefit
Feeling of joy	Personal	Experiential benefit
Self-esteem	Personal/social	Symbolic benefit

Irony of the symbolic benefit

The humour in the popular English TV-series *Keeping up Appearances* is mainly based upon an irony about the symbolic benefits. The suburban elderly housewife Hyacinth Bucket (or 'Bouquet' as she insists), does not feel comfortable in the middle-class society where she always has lived, and to where she really belongs. She admires highly the aristocratic people and their assumed excellent manners, and would like to be seen as an equal. With her pursuits in conducting better manners, she reveals in a quite funny way both the egocentric and social dimension of building up self-esteem.

Core benefits

We looked at the concept of the core benefits earlier, on page 8. The traditional definition is that the product or service contains a key benefit which makes the consumer buy the product. When we stick to the idea that the benefits are the same as the terminal values we encounter a conflict. Namely, the idea of the value of the system and its impact on decision-making is not compatible with the definition of the core benefits. According to Rokeach (1973), the choices we have are based upon the entire system of values, and not just a single value. If you look at your own purchasing decisions, we can recognize that many of our decisions include several benefits at the same time. Of course, these benefits can have different weight values, but the sum of the benefits may be more important than a single benefit. That is, if the whole system of values is said to guide our choices, respectively, purchasing decisions should be based upon the sum of benefits.

When reflecting upon all of the benefits, we can recognize that achieving a feeling of inner harmony, a feeling of satisfaction, and a feeling of happiness requires fulfilment of other necessary benefits. These three terminal values seem to represent the end point of the process. Therefore, I suggest that these should be regarded as the core benefits.

Definition of core benefits

The core benefits are the feeling of inner harmony, the feeling of satisfaction, and the feeling of happiness, since these represent the end point of the benefit processes.

Feeling of inner harmony

Good conscience, self-acceptance, and acceptance of others, are characteristic of a person who is likely to experience a feeling of inner harmony. For maintaining the feeling of inner harmony we want to avoid things that can lead to stress, anxiety, a bad conscience, or a sense of shame.

Feeling of satisfaction

A feeling of satisfaction arises when we have all that is necessary, or have achieved our goal.

Feeling of happiness

In general, we consider the basis and measure of happiness our life situation, and the quality of our relationships. Materialistic things can also be the basis for happiness, but we can feel very happy without fulfilling all the materialistic needs and wants.

3 The materialistic sources of benefits

The features of tangible and intangible products

Back in the 1970s, already a number of academic articles suggested that the sources of benefits are in the features of a product's and a service's properties. The products can be divided into two categories - tangible and intangible. All the physical products are tangible. Intangible products are such as insurance, cleaning services, maintenance and repair, hairdressing, and consultancy services. Although intangible products are often associated with the word 'service', they are not the same thing as customer service. Customer service is our willingness and our capability to serve our customers, to which we return when we look at the benefits of social resources.

Tangible and intangible products form the materialistic dimension.

Tangible products	Intangible products
• All physical products	• insurances • freight services • maintenance and repair • cleaning service • hairdressing • lawyer services • consultancy services, etc. *Intangible products are often services, but they are not the same thing as customer service.*

All products, both tangible and intangible, are made up of a myriad of features. A feature is any trait of the product. The features include for example, the width, height, length and colour. Furthermore, the products are often made from a variety of raw materials, each of which provide a wide range of properties such as weight, strength, flexibility, elasticity, flavour, and fragrance, etc. The price of a product or a service is also a feature even if it does not have the above-mentioned kind of physical characteristics.

An augmented product is an augmentation connected to the product by the manufacturer, merchant or seller. It can also be a natural augmentation, such as the environment where the product is used. An augmented product can also be a source of benefits. They provide numerous opportunities for differentiation, which can be crucial to the success of a product or service. Examples of augmented products are the product range, uses, gifts, exchange, operating instructions, and guidance, maintenance and repair, technical support, and product warranty. The augmented product can also be intangible, such as an idol or a social community.

The advantages of a product

The advantages of a product can derive from the product features and the augmented product. And, as we can well understand, even relatively simple products can contain a large number of features which, separately or together, can give rise to a variety of advantages. As a result, the advantages are significantly less in number than the features.

The definition of a product advantage

An advantage is what features, the augmented product, and the usage of a product produces.

Since the advantages and benefits are traditionally seen as same, their separation can be difficult. The advantages are, however, never emotions such as benefits. For example, advantages are money saving, a car's rapid acceleration or short braking distance, the attractive colour of a mobile phone, etc.

4 The sources of benefits in logistics

A product or a service can provide a number of benefits needed by our customers, but the benefits will not be realized unless the product or service is not readily available when it is needed. Reliable deliveries are always important, because it is one of the most significant reasons for the failure of losing a trade and a customer. Therefore, the compatible of supply chain operations including fast and flexible co-operation are the cornerstones of successful trading for all supply-chain companies. An equally important factor is the cost-efficiency across the supply chain, which enables the profitability in intense competition. Hence, the actors in a supply chain tend to prefer long-term cooperation in order to jointly develop efficient logistics.

Karrus (2005) defines logistics as follows:

The definition of logistics

Logistics is the comprehensive management and the development of material, information, and capital flows, procurement, production, distribution and recycling, maintenance and support, storage, freight, and other services that provide added value to customer service and customer relationships.

As we can detect from the definition, logistics deals with processes and services related to a product. We have previously studied how advantages and the benefits can be derived from the product and service features. In logistics, it is possible to derive advantages and benefits in the same way. These advantages and benefits are particularly important in the business-to-business environment. Therefore, a seller must have a good knowledge of the logistics both within his or her company and the customer's company. And he or she must realize the potential of competitive advantages in logistics.

The flows in logistics

In the logistics, the sources of benefits can be found in three different flows:

- flow of information;
- flow of materials;
- flow of capital.

The flow of information includes all necessary data about the product, production, suppliers, customers, purchasing orders, and customer orders and deliveries. A proper management of data in the flow of information is mandatory in order to efficiently manage the flow of materials and the flow of capital.

The flow of materials includes, for example, the handling of raw materials, components and goods in production and reprocessing, procurement and handling of goods, distribution and recycling in the supply chain.

The flow of capital includes financing and all the transactions. For example, terms of payment, payment discounts, and customer bonuses are factors related to the flow of capital.

Information, material and capital flows are in constant interaction with each other and depend on each other. The efficient management of production control, purchasing, order processing, storage, transportation, and administration requires a seamless coordination.

The advantages in logistics

The advantages in logistics can be derived from the features in the flows.

The definition of advantages in logistics

An advantage in logistics is how a solution in the information flow, material flow, or capital flow can improve the performance in the supply chain and thereby help our customer.

5 The social sources of benefits

Although our products and our logistics can offer a large number of benefits wanted by a customer, even the best product, and the most efficient logistic will rarely sell itself – the willingness and capability of an individual or a group to serve the customers, is the key factor for profitable sales. Thus, the benefits derived from social sources have a very big impact upon the competitive climate and the customers' will to buy the product from our company.

Customer service

As we noted earlier, services are intangible products. But services are not the same thing as customer service. Customer service is a face-to-face interaction with our customer, or through a medium, such as phone, e-mail, etc. In other words, we can provide customer service without encountering our customer face-to-face. Besides the sales people, all the employees in a company are also involved in the customer service. They are just invisible from the customer. This insight is important in order to provide the customer benefits expected from a good customer service.

Definition of customer service

Customer service is the willingness and capability of an individual or a group to serve customers.

Instrumental values

Our willingness and our capability to serve our customers are based upon our instrumental values. Instrumental values, and the sources of instrumental values, that is, our culture and our environment, our personality, our up-bringing, our education and experience, are the social sources of benefits. Our instrumental values constantly form our willingness and capability to act. Parents teach their children instrumental values and emphasize the importance of acting accordingly.

We've already learned that instrumental values can be divided into two categories – moral values and knowledge values. According to Rokeach (1973), the difference can be recognized by identifying the feeling that we experience when we fail to comply, or when we are unable to comply with these values. The moral values will result in bad conscience and the knowledge values in a sense of shame. I think this division involves two problems. First of all, it can be difficult to distinguish moral values and competence values clearly from each other since bad conscience and sense of shame are very similar feelings. And it could be possible to sense both of them at the same time, which does not help us in distinguishing them. Also, cultural differences may affect our ability to distinguish between moral values and knowledge values. Second, dividing the instrumental values in only two groups is quite rough; it does not provide a constructive structure. Hence, I think Rokeach's presentation is not well suited for a commercial context. The purpose is to identify quickly and easily which are the instrumental values that lead to customer benefits. Therefore, dividing the instrumental values in some other way would be justified. That's why I have rejected Rokeach's structure and divided the instrumental values in five groups according to the characteristics of each value. These groups are the attitude values, behaviour values, reliability values, and knowledge values. As the fifth group, I have added values which have become important during the last few decades - environmental values. Furthermore, I have separated the instrumental values of 'Ambitious (hard-working, forward-looking)' and 'Proficient (competent, effective)' and added to the list six instrumental values – empathy, humility, a good listener, friendly, justice, and interaction skills. The instrumental values have been accordingly listed in the following table.

Attitude values
Hard-working and active
Open-minded
Self-discipline
Ambitious and forward-looking
Determined and courageous
Behaviour values
Forgiving
Helpful
Empathic
Joyful
Polite and attentive
Good listener
Humble
Neat and clean
Sympathetic
Friendly
Reliability values
Honest, sincere and truthful
Fair
Dutiful
Responsible and keeping your word
Faithful to yourself and others
Trusting others
Knowledge values
Skilled and proficient
Efficient use of time and process management
Interaction skills
Reasonable and intelligent
Creative and imaginative
Consistent and rational
Environmental values
Saving and rational usage of natural resources
Protecting the environment from pollution

Attitude values

All productive activity is based on the attitude. Without having a good attitude it is difficult to achieve anything. With a good attitude it is possible to replace the shortcomings in other areas.

Behaviour values

Behaviour is always visible and reveals our character traits for others. We can utilize behaviour to establish a good relationship, because we like to deal with nice people. Our behaviour can also raise reliability and credibility. For example, we should always pay special attention when creating the first impression, since the first impression can be made only once, and changing it can be difficult.

Reliability values

Reliability is necessary so that we can function in a group and the basis of any good long-term cooperation. Building of trust can take years, but it can be lost in a matter of seconds. Reconstruction can be very difficult, if not impossible. Thus, reliability is the most valuable intangible capital.

Knowledge values

The knowledge values refer to the knowledge and the abilities which we receive through experience and education, but also to our innate talent. For example, managing the negotiation skills and the sales process must be learned, but also continuously trained in a similar way as athletes prepare for their sports performance. Managing all the processes in logistics is equally important. This type of know-how is important for customer service and a major source of benefits in the business-to-business environment. We need to understand our customers' organization, operation, environment and objectives, too. We must also have a good view of your customers business, and the factors affecting the development of their business, so that we can continue to operate effectively. And of course we have to know our products and our competitors, as well as their products and practices. These are the challenges which nobody can manage alone. An efficient management of the processes in logistics and the continuous development of these processes require a well-organized input from the whole organization. This in turn requires that the company's management has a good ability. Finally, it should be noted that culture is also a source for instrumental values. Therefore, we must learn the culture of the country where we operate, so that we can succeed outside our own familiar environment.

Environmental values

Concerns about the development of our common environment have changed our values. Therefore, we expect that environmental issues should always be considered in all activities. Our customers are not interested in only the product itself, but also in how it is produced. Our customers' behaviour shows that environmental values are a source of benefits. Companies require that all natural resources are used sparingly. For example, organic products have become increasingly popular. We need to prevent the climate change. We need to protect our water and our soil from pollution. Noise must be reduced. But also animals should be treated appropriately. Use of animal tests in R&D is not accepted. Domestic animals should be treated well.

Environmental values are essential for business today, and these are seen more often as an opportunity rather than a threat.

6 The model for identifying customer benefits

The model for identifying customer benefits is a tool that makes it possible to easily and quickly identify any benefits provided by the products and services as well as logistics and customer service.

The structure of the model

The structure of the model for identifying customer benefits describes a four-step process. The base is the source level. The source level is divided into three parts; materialistic, logistical, and social. The materialistic part includes the features of a tangible and intangible product and the augmented product. The logistical part includes the features of the flows in logistics. The social part includes the sources of instrumental values, i.e., up-bringing, education, and experience, personality, culture, and the environment.

The second step is the rational level. The rational level is divided into three parts in the same way as the source level. The materialistic part includes the advantages derived from the tangible and intangible product, and the augmented product. The logistical part includes the advantages derived from the flows in logistics. The social part includes the instrumental values.

The third step is the emotional level including all the ten benefits in their groups. Here the processes coming from the source and rational level join together.

The fourth step of the process is the core level including the three core benefits; feeling of inner harmony, feeling of satisfaction, and feeling of happiness.

The number of factors changes from level to level. In the source level, the factors are infinite in number. In the rational level, there are still a myriad of factors. At the emotional level, the number of factors has been reduced to ten and, ultimately, in the core level there are only three factors. All the possible processes end up always with the same result.

The number of factors in the source level and rational level indicates that the possible processes are also countless in number. At the same time, it is important to note that one process can lead several benefits, and many different processes can lead to the same benefit. In other words, the processes may develop into a very complex and dense network at the source and rational level, but the processes thin out significantly at the emotional level ending at the core level in only the three core benefits.

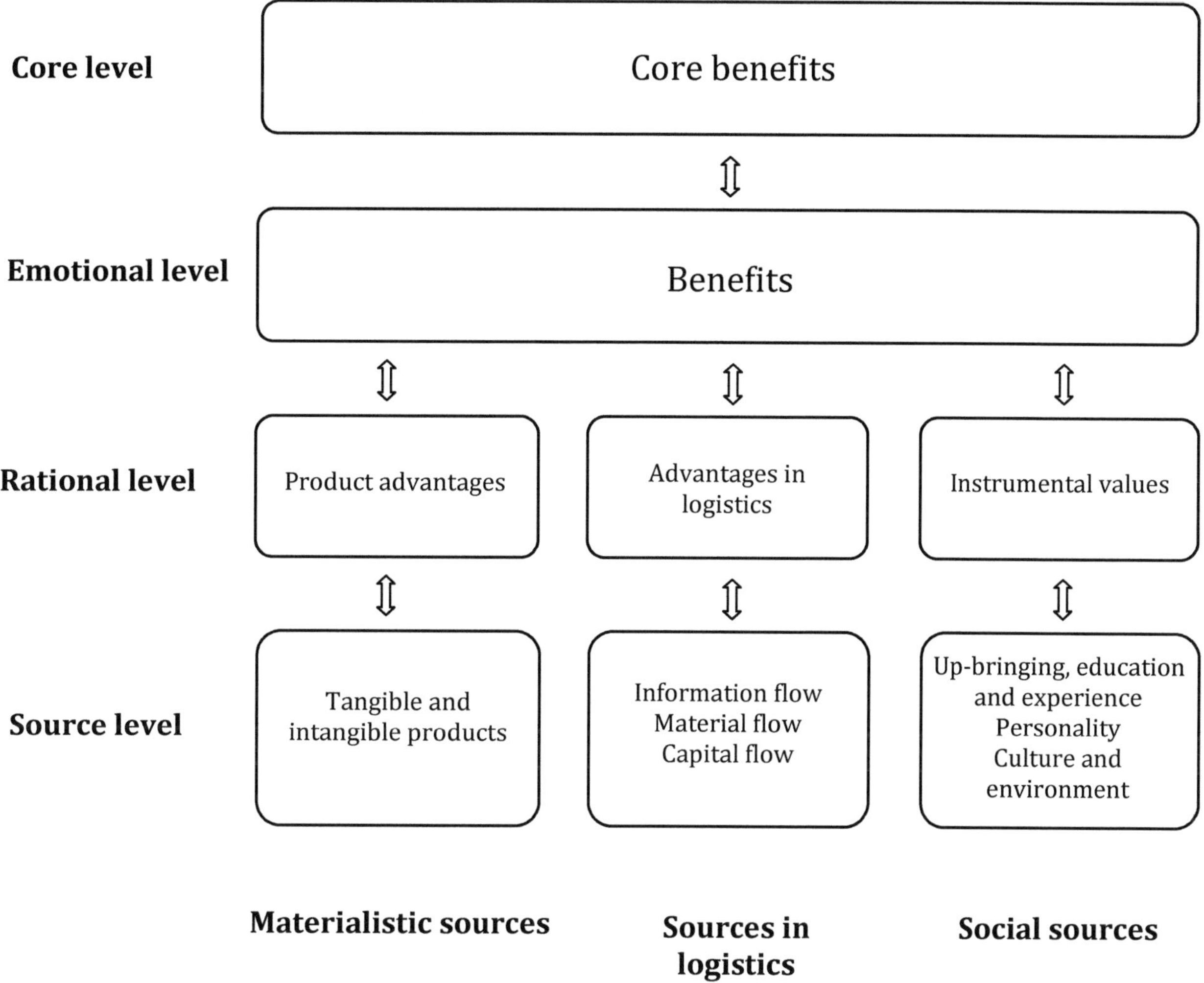

The model can be utilized in two directions. By starting from the source level towards the core level, it is possible to identify all the potential advantages and benefits. When designing our market communication, or product argumentation, however, we need to choose the opposite direction, that is, start from the benefits. Our customers buy the benefits and therefore they are always interested in the benefits. The source and rational level represents the evidence of the benefits. In other words, there is very little sense to present evidence unless our customer understands what we are intending to testify. Not to mention, of course, that we are aware what benefits our customers need.

The difference of being customer-oriented versus product-oriented

In the model, the source level and the rational level represent product-oriented thinking. Here the features and advantages of the products and the service are in the focus. When we extend our thinking up to the emotional level, we become customer-oriented. Here we are able us to see the positive feelings that our customers need and want to experience. In other words, the emotional level and the core level represent customer-oriented thinking.

References

The model for identifying customer benefits includes elements from Futrell's FAB-model (1984, 2006) and Gutman Means-End Chain Model (1982), as well as Rokeach (1973) ideas of human values. I have added my idea of core benefits. The elements in logistics are based on the book *Logistiikka* written by Karrus. The grouping of instrumental values has been gathered from various sources. The grouping of benefits has been selected from various sources such as Sheth, Newman and Gross (1991), Aaker (1996), Park, Jaworski and MacInnis (1986). The augmented product is based on the ideas of Theodor Levitt (1980). Definitions of key terms are adjusted to fit the context.

The model for identifying customer benefits

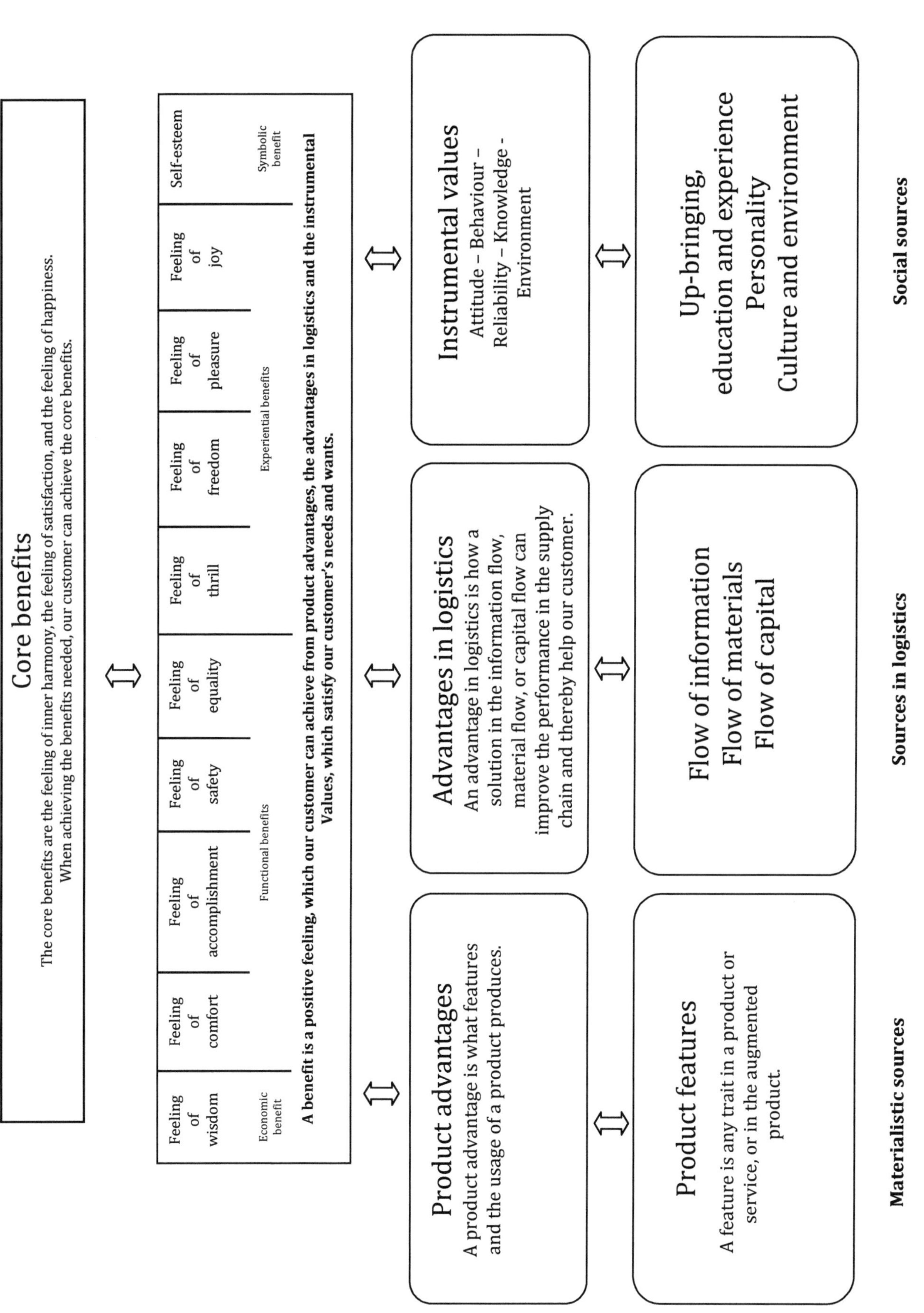

7 Theses and definitions

Definition of benefits
A benefit is a positive feeling, which our customer can achieve from product advantages, the advantages in logistics and the instrumental values, which satisfy our customer's needs and wants.

Five theses of customer benefits

1. All the benefits are positive feelings, which we try to continuously consciously and unconsciously achieve. Feelings are not static or measurable.
2. Benefits are a result of numerous processes, which can be derived from materialistic sources, sources in logistics and social sources. Processes can be divided into four levels. These are the source level, rational level, emotional level and the core level.
3. Benefits can be divided into two levels according to the order they emerge. There are ten benefits and three core benefits. In sociology, all these benefits are called terminal values. The core benefits are the feeling of inner harmony, the feeling of satisfaction and the feeling of happiness. The benefits are the feeling of wisdom, the feeling of comfort, the feeling of accomplishment, the feeling of safety, the feeling of equality, the feeling of thrill, the feeling of pleasure, the feeling of freedom, the feeling of joy, and self esteem. The terminal values salvation, true friendship and love are excluded due to ethical and legal reasons.
4. Benefits can be divided into four groups; economic benefits, functional benefits, experiential benefits, and symbolic benefits.
5. Benefits are always subjective, that is, each customer experiences the benefits in their own way.

Benefits and added value

So far, we have received answers to the most essential questions regarding customer benefits. We know what a benefit is, how many benefits there are, and how they can be grouped, how benefits can be achieved, and how we can present evidence about identified benefits. But the model for identifying benefits also provides a good basis for the definition of added value.

Added value can be obtained from the model, as well as the materialistic and social dimensions of sources and processes. Added value is any change in the source level and rational level in the model. It is important to note, however, that the added value is valid only when a customer recognizes the change as an improvement to a relevant benefit. Otherwise, the change may be only an additional cost, which undermines the profitability of the company.

Definition of added value

Added value is any change in the source level or rational level, which the customer recognises as an improvement in a relevant benefit for the customer.

Benefits and a brand

In general, a trademark and a brand are seen as the same thing, that is, as the name or mark by which a product can be identified. In marketing, however, there is a significant difference between a trademark and a brand. The company can launch a trademark, but a brand must be earned, because the status of the brand is given by customers. In other words, when a product or service rises to a level where the customer feels that the trademark solely provides added value to the customer, a trademark has advanced to a brand. From the perspective of customer benefits, a brand can thus be defined as follows.

Definition of a brand

A brand is a warranty – a product or a service which by its trade mark, name, or logo is capable to assure that its benefits are always fulfilled.

According to this definition a product or service includes benefits, valued and wanted by the customer. Hence, a brand is a warranty, assuring that its benefits are always fulfilled. Due to the fact that the brand status is always given by the customers, it is interesting to note that the warranty is not provided by the manufacturer or seller, but the customer.

Any of the benefits of the product or service may alone or in combination be the foundation for the brand. In other words, a brand does not have to be a high-status product. For example, even the most affordable option can provide the feeling of the wisdom, which can be a foundation for a brand status.

In this context, it is also important to note that a brand is not the same as image. We may have many products or services with very positive image. But positive image does not necessarily make the product or service a brand. Only when the positive image of a product or service becomes in line with the above definition, it becomes a brand. That is, image is perception of something, not the brand-like insurance of a product or service benefits realization. The means of developing brand identity, or developing good image, however, are very similar.

8 Communicating benefits

In order to effectively communicate benefits, it is important to understand the location of our object, that is, where the market is. At the same time, it is important that the message is customer-oriented. Our understanding of customer benefits and choosing customer benefits as the main theme in our message, create the conditions for good results. I will now present a number of my thoughts.

Market

Market is one of the most frequent words in media. The word market is used in many different contexts, but it is not always entirely clear where the market is although it affects strongly all our lives. No wonder, since the word market may mean at least eight different things.

1. Market is target groups and target situations. A target group can be a specific demographic group, or a group of people living in a certain area, which is recognized by the marketer to be their potential customers. Target situations are specific situations raising needs that are identified in advance. For example, leaving your car for service can raise a need for renting a car.

2. Market is a trading place where people gather to buy and sell, such as a market, a bazaar, an auction, a kiosk, a shop, shopping halls, shops, a supermarket, a department store, a mall, a stock exchange, and a trade fair.

3. Market is distribution systems, such as direct sales, retail, wholesale, renting, auctions, mail order, and the Internet. For example, as a distributions system Internet is capable of transmitting digital products and services such as computer programmes, trips, music, and interactive services.

4. Market is a product group, a sector, or a segment. For example, a lot of news is expected in the mobile phone market, prices have increased in the dairy product markets, and the bicycles market is most active in the spring. Or the automotive sector and the forest industry are in decline, while domestic tourism has increased. In many technical fields, the market is divided into two segments – the OEM market and after-market.

5. Market is dates and time periods. The Christmas market is vital for retailers. After Christmas, the winter sale season starts, the tourist and holiday season is in summer, Mother's Day is important for florists.

6. Market is a myriad of actors creating a network. Companies try to connect with other companies which they feel to be important for their business. When working together, companies can strengthen their position in the market.

7. Market is the place where all the decisions are made. Hence, the market is located in the mind of our present and potential customers. And in the mind of all the persons that may affect our present and potential customers' decisions. The market is physically located in between the ears of the mentioned persons. Brain researchers might be able to show even a more precise location, but I believe that this address is accurate enough. We can also be sure that these markets have always been located at this address, and their migration is not likely despite the technological advances.

8. Market is the national economy. In this case, we talk about the market at a higher conceptual level. In the national economy we can see how the interaction of supply and demand rules business, economies, employment, and other economic factors.

In order to understand customer benefits, the seventh option is the only correct approach. All purchase decisions, both good and bad, are the result of our customers' ideas. This is true for both B2B and B2C environments. That's why our message must be directed precisely towards the area, which is located behind the brow bone of the people in the target group. We must endeavour to clarify our customers' thoughts as they tell us very much about our customers' needs and wants. Well-placed questions and listening are by far the best tools for this. And this is the hallmark of a skilled and hard-working seller.

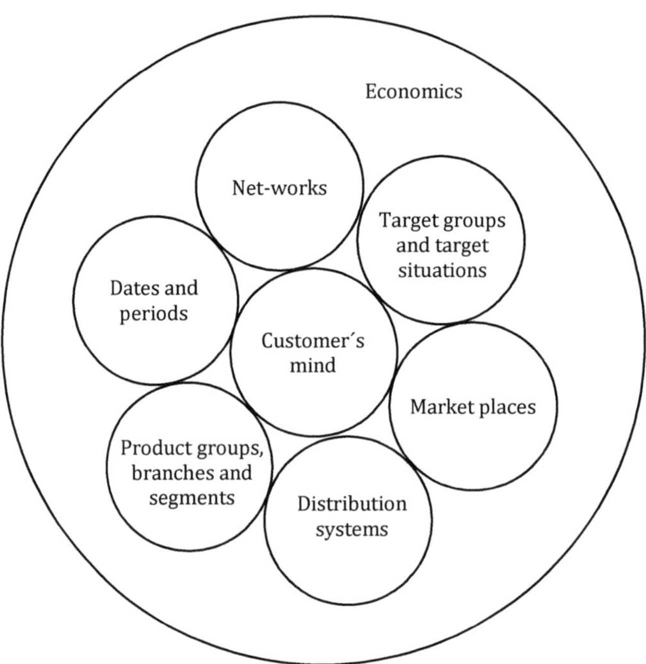

The word market can mean at least eight different things. In order to understand the customer benefits, the most important market is located in the customer's mind, due to the fact that it's the place where all the decisions are made.

Benefits and positioning

Positioning is the customer's perception of a product and a pre-determined idea of a company to achieve a desired positioning of its product or service. Hence, the factors that influence the positioning are emphasized in market communication. Let us assume that the market has two competing products. One of them is regarded as safe, and the other as sporty. A third competing product will now appear in the market. If the company builds up its communication in a way that their new product will be positioned to one of the existing category, the new product will not clearly stand out from the crowd. It would be more beneficial to design a message for the new product, which would create a new attractive perception in the customer's mind. The product, of course, must be in accordance with the positioning in order to establish and maintain the desired perception.

The benefits of a product or service and their processes, as well as all the instrumental values are a versatile and a customer-oriented basis for planning a positioning. By combining the benefits, it is possible to find a number of new positioning options. Too many factors, however, may result in confusion. Therefore, only a couple of good factors could be enough for a proper differentiation. In addition, combining many factors may prevent the required clarity and lead to a very high standard deviation of the customer's perceptions. The positioning is successful when most of the customers have an equal perception, and when this perception meets the company's objectives.

Achieving the desired perceptions requires always resolute and consistent market communication, and a lot of time. When the customers have eventually created a perception of a product or service, changing it is very difficult. Therefore, the positioning of a product or service must be carefully planned, and the long-term effects must also be taken into account.

Benefits and advertising

The Italian clothing brand Benetton carried out in the 1980's an exceptional and much-debated campaign. The campaign ads did not present the company's products, but rather visually striking images were used, which were praised as artistic. In terms of attracting attention, Benetton's campaign was a great success. In contrast, the campaign's impact on the company's product sales was not as expected – quite the contrary. Benetton stopped the odyssey and returned to their original style of advertising.

I think that Benetton's campaign is an excellent example of the fact that drawing attention is not the same as selling advertising. Drawing attention is actually quite easy. But to draw attention and increase the demand for the product at the same time, is a much more challenging skill. The content of an ad, as well as how and where the ad is presented, has always an impact to the result. Therefore, the often heard phrase "it is not important what is written about us, as long as we are seen on the pages" is a very dangerous precept.

Generally, it can be stated that before preparing an ad, it is important to see the benefits of the product or service. It is equally important to see the features and advantages that lead to these benefits, as well as the instrumental values appreciated by the people in the target group. If these things are not known and well structured, the ad may become, at worst, an incoherent jumble.

In order to reach the market, in this case our customer's mind, we must present our message in a suitable way. First of all, the path entering our customer's mind pass hearing, vision, smell, taste and touch senses. Therefore, the message needs to be designed in such a way that it will stick to the senses. Second, the message has to differentiate from the thousands of other commercial messages that our customers face every day. This requires that the message content has to be interesting. And what could be more interesting from the customer's point of view than to tell clearly the benefits of the product or service in a pleasant way? There are, however, situations where it is necessary to present the features and advantages at the same time with benefits. When our customer wants to compare available options, his or her attention is focused on measurable factors, that is, the features and benefits. For example, many technical products highlight the advantages and features, and emphasize the superior number of features. And of course, price is a factor that must be presented for comparison. Please remember that added value is any change in the source or a rational level that the customer understands as a positive impact on the benefits. It is therefore important that we are aware of the benefits and all the processes leading to them, and the benefits that our customers appreciate.

When designing an advertisement, with the purpose of influencing our customers' willingness to purchase and to make the choices we want, we should consider how the benefits could be delivered. All the media don't have the same capabilities to raise various types of emotions. Sometimes even the best advertising is not enough; the customer must be offered the opportunity to test the product or service in practice. For example, car dealers often send invitations to trials, free samples are given out for testing, and stores arrange tasting campaigns.

Benefits are positive feelings that our customers want to be always able to experience. On the other hand, advantages and features are the evidence of the benefits. But we can often see ads, which only provide evidence! It is possible, of course, that benefits are so obvious, or the purpose is to highlight the features and advantages in order to facilitate a comparison. But why leave out the benefits? I think a good advertisement always attracts attention, and at the same time expresses positive feelings, that is, the benefits that the product or service can deliver. Our customers are always interested in the benefits of a product or service. Therefore, benefits should have a priority, that is, the ad should always give an answer to the question, "What's in it for me?" At the same time, of course, it is essential that our customers will remember the ad. A good context helps remembering. The ad context can be built from the evidence, the advantages and features of the product, as well as the instrumental values appreciated by the customer.

Benefits and selling

As a seller, we must be aware of the benefits of our products or services and their processes. We must remember at all times to comply with the instrumental values that our customers appreciate. In the dialogue with our customers, we must place well thought out questions and study what our customers need and what things they appreciate. We need to listen to our customers and to demonstrate that we are listening. If necessary, we need to set more questions and continue to listen to our customers. Customers value sellers who are interested in their situation, needs and wants. A successful dialogue often leads naturally to a good result.

After mapping the customer's situation, we can present the benefits of your product or service in an appropriate order and, if necessary, use the advantages and features of the product or service as evidence. It is important to recognize, however, that the advantages and features can in some cases be more important than the benefit. First of all with products, which are compared with each other, the superiority assessment is carried out by comparing the relevant measurable factors, i.e., the advantages and features. Second, our clients may have difficulties in seeing the difference between two products. Then our customer's decision may be based on the number of features, although much of it would be practically irrelevant factors. Third, the price including all matters related to the total cost must always be presented clearly, when our customer puts financial gain first. Remember that feelings cannot be measured, and therefore they are not comparable.

A sales man has two ears and one mouth.

When interacting with a customer, these should be used vis-à-vis.

In B2B, our customers can buy the product for many different reasons. First of all, in order to sell it forward as it is (distribution), second, to use it for production (investment, raw material, component, and energy). Third, procurements are needed for the daily needs such as office supplies, detergents, etc. Benefits associated with the logistics are essential to the B2B, that is, factors relating to the payment and delivery terms and conditions, purchase orders, manufacturing, method of delivery, in terms of capacity and reliability, product selection, delivery volumes, and inventory turnover, packaging and recycling. Therefore, in B2B the seller must also master the basics of logistics and be able to calculate the key financial indicators.

9 Identifying benefits

Product benefits and their processes

It is possible to identify customer benefits and their processes in any product and service benefits. The best source of information is, of course, the customer, but also the sales people often possess experience which can be used in determining benefits.

The benefits of a Kickbike

The Kickbike scooter is a versatile vehicle for physical activity, and can be considered as a High-Involvement product. It can be used to generate useful exercise, fitness, hiking as well as competition. The customer benefits of the Kickbike scooter have been resolved. Below are the benefits and their processes.

Economic benefits and their processes

Feature (source level)	Advantage (rational level)	Benefit (emotional level)
Price	Attractive price	Feeling of wisdom
Cost of usage	Low maintenance costs	Feeling of wisdom
Travelling costs	Savings in travelling costs	Feeling of wisdom

Functional benefits and their processes

Feature (source level)	Advantage(rational level)	Benefit (emotional level)
Dimensions, weight, and design	Easy to start	Feeling of comfort
Low footboard and design	Easy and fast to get moving	Feeling of comfort
Dimensions, weight, and design	Easy to handle and use	Feeling of comfort
Dimensions, weight, and design	Easy to handle and use in a crowd	Feeling of comfort
Dimensions, weight, and design	Practical utility vehicle	Feeling of comfort
Dimensions, weight, and design	A practical combination of a training tool and a utility vehicle	Feeling of comfort
Number of components and design	Little maintenance and easy to maintain	Feeling of comfort
Dimensions, weight, and design	Easy and practical to transport	Feeling of comfort
Low footboard and design	Easy to keep balance	Feeling of safety
Dimensions, weight, and design	Lightweight, comfortable, and practical training tool	Feeling of comfort
Design	Provides diverse training	Feeling of accomplishment
Design	Provides good condition and strength	Feeling of accomplishment
Design	Supplemental training to other sports	Feeling of accomplishment
Design	Suitable also for overweight people and people with injuries	Feeling of comfort/accomplishment
Design	A good rehabilitation tool for certain injuries	Feeling of comfort/accomplishment

Experiential benefits and their benefits

Feature (source level)	Advantage (rational level)	Benefit (emotional level)
The augmented product	Fine design and beautiful colours	Feeling of pleasure
Design	An exciting driving experience	Feeling of joy/thrill
The augmented product	Reactions and comments from other people	Feeling of joy
Design	Refreshing variation	Feeling of pleasure
Design	Easy to observe the environment and enjoy it	Feeling of pleasure
The augmented product	A break free from the daily grind	Feeling of freedom
The augmented product	Get-together with other bikers	Feeling of joy

Symbolic benefits and their processes

Feature (source level)	Advantage (rational level)	Benefit (emotional level)
The augmented product	Accompanied by idols	Self-esteem through fellowship
The augmented product	Get-together with other bikers	Self-esteem through fellowship
The augmented product	Get-together with your family	Self-esteem through fellowship
The augmented product	Achieving victories in competition	Self-esteem through respect

The Kickbike scooter offers as many as nine customer benefits - feeling of wisdom, comfort, accomplishment, safety, joy, thrill, pleasure and freedom, and self-esteem. Regarding benefits the product is quite diverse. It can give the user a sense of well-being in many ways.

Building the processes

It is possible that you identify first a benefit of a product or service. Then you can use the model to determine the sources of the benefit. For example, it is possible that we feel that a product is comfortable. In other words, we identify first the benefit. The model provides the possibility to identify the process that leads to the feeling of comfort. Or, if you know that a car has a short braking distance. Then we can find out what features provide the advantage and the benefit that this advantage can lead to.

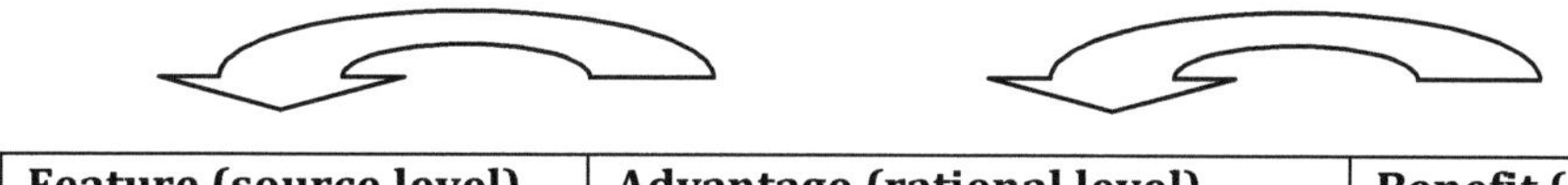

Feature (source level)	Advantage (rational level)	Benefit (emotional level)
?	?	Feeling of comfort
?	Short braking distance	?

In the following are five examples of how the process flow can be resolved.

1. Price, economical or expensive, is a feature of a product or a service. The possibility of saving money is an advantage. When we choose an economical option and save, we feel that we are wise. Feeling of wisdom is a benefit. The lowest price is not always an option to save the most. One of the more expensive options can be much more durable and last longer. Or a more expensive alternative with lower operating costs over time, can lead to significant savings. The price of a product or service alone does not always tell us which option will ultimately lead to the best choice. But when we have seen the effort to find the best deal, and save even more money, we can feel very wise. Also, the timing of the acquisition can evoke a sense of wisdom. If we wait until the sales, we can save money, and feel ourselves wiser than the others.

Feature (source level)	Advantage (rational level)	Benefit (emotional level)
Price (economical)	Savings	Feeling of wisdom
Price/quality ratio	Durable and lasting – savings over time	Feeling of wisdom
Cost of usage	Small cost	Feeling of wisdom

2. A hair salon service – a loyalty card can provide the opportunity to save money. Saving money is an advantage. The feeling of wisdom, in turn, is what we obtain from saving our money. The furnishing consists of numerous features. The advantage of these can be a pleasant environment and atmosphere. The benefit derived from these is the feeling of pleasure. The various hairdresser devices can have a wide range of features. Soft seats are an advantage. The benefit is the feeling of comfort. The adjustability of the equipment is also another advantage leading to the feeling of comfort. Shampoos and other care products also consist of many features. A good smell is an advantage, and the benefit is the feeling of pleasure. In addition, these agents can be tested and mild, which is an advantage. These things can evoke a feeling of safety, which is a benefit. An advantage of a hair salon visit, may be a momentary break from the everyday grind, giving the feeling of freedom as a benefit. Besides the loyalty card, augmented products can also be free coffee, magazines, and music, which consist of many features. Good-tasting coffee, interesting articles and relaxing music are the advantages. Their benefit is the feeling of pleasure. When the work of the skilled hairdresser leads to a desired result, the benefit is the feeling of accomplishment and self-esteem. Thus, a hair salon service can provide at least seven benefits – feelings of wisdom, comfort, freedom, accomplishment, safety and pleasure, as well as self-esteem.

Feature (source level)	Advantage (rational level)	Benefit (emotional level)
Loyalty card	Discount from list prices	Feeling of wisdom
Interior	Pleasant environment and atmosphere	Feeling of pleasure
Padded seat	Soft surface	Feeling of comfort
Aromatic products	Good smell	Feeling of pleasure
Tested products	No risk of allergic reactions	Feeling of safety
Rare	A break from the daily grind	Feeling of freedom
Free coffee	Tasty and good smell	Feeling of pleasure
Magazines	Interesting articles	Feeling of pleasure
Music	Relaxing	Feeling of pleasure
Skilful hair dresser	Good looking haircut	Self-esteem

3. The features of a puzzle include a picture, the dimension of the puzzle, and the number of pieces and their shape. The purpose of a puzzle is to put the pieces together correctly – the advantage is to find a solution. It can evoke a feeling of accomplishment every time a piece finds the right place. Not to mention the feeling of accomplishment when the puzzle is eventually completed. And a feeling of accomplishment is the benefit. During the assembly, we have to constantly look for solutions – the advantage is a meaningful reflection. This reflection may lead to benefits such as feeling of thrill, feeling of joy, and feeling of pleasure. The puzzle image can be beautiful, which is an advantage. This can also lead to a feeling of pleasure. The augmented product of a puzzle can be a group of friends that have come together for solving the puzzle. The advantage is the possibility of interaction. The benefit derived from the interaction can be a sense of social, belonging, which strengthens our self-esteem. In addition, during the interaction, we can experience joy and a feeling of equality that are benefits. Consequently, a puzzle can offer at least six benefits – feelings of accomplishment, thrill, joy, pleasure, equality, and strengthen our self-esteem.

Feature (source level)	Advantage (rational level)	Benefit (emotional level)
Numerous pieces	Pleasant reflection	Feeling of pleasure
The augmented product	Fun	Feeling of joy
Numerous pieces	Looking for a solution	Feeling of thrill
Numerous pieces	Finding a solution	Feeling of accomplishment
A picture	A beautiful picture	Feeling of pleasure
The augmented product	Everyone can participate	Feeling of equality
The augmented product	Get-together	Self-esteem

4. A home insurance is an intangible product. The features of insurance are its terms and conditions. Damages that the insurance covers provide financial protection and saving of our money. These are, in turn, the advantages of insurance. Insurance benefits are, therefore, a feeling of safety and a feeling of wisdom. Also, the design of an insurance website includes many features. When these features suit us well, it can be convenient to review of the insurance policy, buy insurance, and make a damage report. These are the advantages. The feeling of comfort is a benefit derived from these benefits. Various types of insurance, the concentration of the same company may give a discount on insurance premiums, which is an advantage. Wisdom is feeling the benefits derived from this. Insurances can also include augmented products, which can be a source for other advantages and benefits.

Feature (source level)	Advantage (rational level)	Benefit (emotional level)
Terms and conditions	Protection from financial problems	Feeling of safety
Terms and conditions	Saving money	Feeling of wisdom
Web site	Easy to shop	Feeling of comfort
Terms and conditions	Special discount	Feeling of wisdom

5. Self-esteem and our struggle to strengthen our self-esteem, relates to two dimensions – egoistic and social. In the egoistic dimension, the importance is about differentiating from others. In the social dimension, emphasis is on the need of belonging to a group. In both cases, a feature is any trait in the product or service, or in the augmented product that evokes a sense of status. It may be, for example, a brand, or an idol associated with the product. Differentiation and belonging are advantages. When we buy a product, considered as a luxury brand, which few others possess, we have the opportunity to stand out from the group. Similarly, we can buy a brand which can connect us to an idol or a group.

The benefits and their processes in logistics

For their operations, companies need a variety of products and services from other companies. Manufacturing companies invest in production machinery and purchase raw materials and supplies to manufacture their products. Distributors buy products and sell them on. For all companies, it is very important that all of their equipment and supply-chain processes work effectively. Indicators include the quality of the processes, order and delivery costs, the reliability of deliveries from suppliers, supply and inventory turnover. The following are examples of the benefits that are derived from the features of the information, the material, and the capital flow. Economic benefits and functional benefits are typical in logistics.

Information flow

Feature (source level)	Advantage (rational level)	Benefit (emotional level)
Order centre for placing orders	Fast processing of orders	Feeling of accomplishment
Order centre for placing orders	Easy to place an order	Feeling of comfort
Technical service	Easy to get required information	Feeling of comfort
Technical service	Easy to get required information	Feeling of accomplishment
Technical service	Reliable data	Feeling of safety
Bar code	Easy to handle	Feeling of comfort
Bar code	Fast processing – savings in time/costs	Feeling of wisdom
Bar code	Correct data	Feeling of safety
Tracking number	Easy to track the delivery	Feeling of comfort
Production number	Possible to identify when manufactured	Feeling of safety
Order acknowledgement	Certainty of received order	Feeling of accomplishment

Material flow

Feature (source level)	Advantage (rational level)	Benefit (emotional level)
One supplier	Savings in purchasing costs	Feeling of wisdom
One supplier	Savings in freight costs	Feeling of wisdom
One supplier	Better terms	Feeling of wisdom
A combined warehouse/wholesale/display box	Savings in handling costs	Feeling of wisdom
A combined warehouse/wholesale/display box	Easy to handle	Feeling of comfort
Quantities according to order	Good inventory turnover	Feeling of wisdom
Safety stock	Instant availability	Feeling of safety
Recyclable box	Less waste – savings in waste costs	Feeling of wisdom
Trolley	Easy to handle	Feeling of comfort
Trolley	Fast to handle – savings in time and costs	Feeling of wisdom
Parking place	Easy to shop	Feeling of comfort
Wide corridors in the store	Easy to move	Feeling of comfort
Wide product range	All at the same time	Feeling of accomplishment
Wide product range	All at once	Feeling of comfort

Capital flow

Feature (source level)	Advantage (rational level)	Benefit (emotional level)
Credit	Interest-free payment	Feeling of wisdom
Bank payment	Easy transaction	Feeling of comfort
Bank payment	Payments in time	Feeling of safety
Bank payment	All manageable with one contract	Feeling of accomplishment

Social benefits and their processes

Our customers always appreciate good customer service. By providing a good customer service, we can therefore achieve a significant competitive advantage. In customer service and in other spheres of life too, we consider values related to attitude fundamental. It is important to recognize that we can all develop our instrumental values. This training has a significant role, especially in the values related to knowledge, which for example, include sales skills. In addition, this category includes product knowledge and our ability to understand our customers' needs and finding solutions to them.

The development of our instrumental values is a constant learning process. They need to be practiced the same way as the athletes who strive to achieve better results do. The assumption that we have already learned everything is very dangerous. Arrogance can then empower our mind, and as a result a constructive learning process becomes more difficult. Remember always the definition of customer service – the individual's and the group's willingness and ability to serve customers. These matters need to be constantly nurtured and developed so that our customers can achieve all the benefits.

The following table shows the attitude, behaviour, integrity, competence, and environmental values and my interpretation of what the customer benefits each value can awake.

Benefits				
Feeling of comfort Feeling of accomplishment Feeling of safety Feeling of freedom	Feeling of comfort Feeling of accomplishment Feeling of safety Feeling of pleasure Feeling of freedom Feeling of joy Self-esteem	Feeling of safety Feeling of equality	Feeling of comfort Feeling of accomplishment Feeling of safety Feeling of pleasure Feeling of freedom	Feeling of wisdom Feeling of safety
⇕	⇕	⇕	⇕	⇕
Attitude values	**Behaviour values**	**Reliability values**	**Knowledge values**	**Environmental values**
Hard-working and active Open-minded Self-discipline Ambitious and forward-looking Determined and courageous	Forgiving Helpful Empathic Joyful Polite and attentive Good listener Humble Neat and clean Sympathetic Friendly	Honest, sincere and truthful Fair Dutiful Responsible and keeping your word Faithful to yourself and others Trusting others	Skilled and proficient Efficient use of time and process management Interaction skills Reasonable and intelligent Creative and imaginative	Saving and rational usage of natural resources Protecting the environment from pollution
Instrumental values				

All the instrumental values can awake the feeling of safety. The feeling of safety is actually one of the most important benefits wanted by our customers. Behaviour values can raise quite a large number of benefits. Although the reliability and environmental values can raise only two benefits, these groups are no less important – on the contrary.

When we encounter a customer, it is difficult to detect if our customers consider some instrumental values more important than others. But a good customer service is always composed of the total, where all the instrumental values play an important part. So, use them in accordance with the situation. Remember that all of the benefits are emotions – and that your customers will always buy benefits. By providing a good customer service, you can always contribute to make your customers interested in buying a product or service from you, instead from your competitor.

To remember

Management

- Study the values of your customers and connect them with your company values.
- Provide your staff a training program for developing instrumental values. Be a good example in following the instrumental values.
- Make a plan for identifying the benefits and their processes of your products.
- Develop the benefits through training, R&D, and by expanding and utilizing your network.

Marketing managers and copywriters

- Identify all the benefits and processes in the product.
- Utilize all the benefits and the processes in designing your marketing message and in planning the positioning of the product. Note the importance of advantages and features in a situation in which the customer is aware of the benefit, and therefore places the decision making in a comparison of advantages and features.
- When planning your marketing message consider what means are best for promoting each benefit. These could be text, pictures, a movie, a trial, or any combination of these. Consider a suitable media at the same time.
- Regarding the context of your marketing message, consider the usage of the product, advantages and benefits.
- Present the benefits and prove them with the advantages and benefits.

Sales people

- Develop and train continuously instrumental values.
- Try always to create a nice atmosphere by using the instrumental values appreciated by your customer.
- Learn the benefits and their processes of your products, services and logistics. Note the importance of advantages and features in a situation in which the customer is aware of the benefit, and therefore places the decision-making in a comparison of advantages and features.
- Make a list of relevant questions and learn to use them properly.
- Clarify the benefits valued by your customer in an early stage of your sales process.
- Listen carefully what your customer tells you, and show that you are listening.
- Present the benefits and prove them with the advantages and benefits.

References

Articles

Agres, Stuart J.; Dubitsky, Tony M. (1996). Changing Needs for Brands, *Journal of Advertising Research*, pp. 21–30.

Bloch, Peter H.; Richins, Marscha L. (1983). A Theoretical Model for the Study of Product Importance Perceptions, *Journal of Marketing*, Vol. 47, Issue 3, pp. 69–81.

Botschen, Günther; Thelen Eva M.; Pieters, Rik (1999). Using means-end structures for benefit segmentation: an application to services, European Journal of Marketing, Vol. 33, No. ½, pp. 38–52.

Green, Paul E.; Wind, Yoram; Jain, Arun K. (1972). Benefit Bundle Analysis, *Journal of Advertising Research,* Vol. 12, Issue 2, p. 31, 6p.

Gutman, Jonathan (1982). A Means-End Chain Model Based on Consumer Categorization Processes, *Journal of Marketing*, Vol. 46 (Spring 1982), pp. 60–72

Gutman, Jonathan (1991). Exploring the Nature of Linkages Between Consequences and Values, *Journal of Business Research*, pp. 143–148.

Haley, Russel I. (1968). Benefit Segmentation: A Decision-oriented Research Tool, *Journal of Marketing*, Vol. 32 (July 1968), pp. 30–35.

Haley, Russel I. (1971). Beyond Benefit Segmentation, *Journal of Advertising Research*, Vol. 11, Issue 4, p. 3, 6p.

Haley, Russel I. (1983). Benefit Segmentation - 20 Years Later, *Journal of Consumer Marketing*, Vol. 1, Issue 2, p. 5, 9p.

Hirschman, Elisabeth C.; Holbrook, Morris B. (1982). Hedonic Consumption: Emerging Concepts, Methods and Propositions, *Journal of Marketing*, 32 (Summer), pp. 30–5.

Johnson, Michael D. (1989). On the Nature of Products Attributes and Attribute Relationships, *Advances in Consumer Research*, Vol. 16, Issue 1, p. 598.

Levitt, Theodore (1980). Marketing Success through Differentiation - of Anything, *Harvard Business Review,* (January–February), pp. 83–91.

Levy, Sidney J. (1959). Symbols for Sale, *Harvard Business Review*, 37 (July–August), pp. 117–119.

Myers, James H. (1976). Benefit Structure Analysis: A New Tool for Product Planning, *Journal of Marketing*, 40 (October), pp. 23–32.

Park, C. Whan; Jaworski, Bernard J.; MacInnis, Deborah J. (October 1986). Strategic Brand Concept-Image Management, *Journal of Marketing* 50: pp. 135–145.

Reynolds, Thomas J.; Gutman, Jonathan (1988). Laddering Theory, Method, Analysis, and Interpretation, *Journal of Advertising Research*, pp. 11–31.

Reynolds, Thomas J.; Gengler Charles E.; Howard Daniel J. (1995). A means-end analysis of brand persuasion through advertising, *International Journal of Research in Marketing*, Vol. 12, Issue 3, p. 257, 10 p.

Sheth, Jagdish N.; Newman, Bruce I.; Gross, Barbara L. (1991). Why We Buy What We Buy: A Theory of Consumption Values, *Journal of Business Research* 22, pp. 159–170.

Siegel, Carolyn F.; Powers Richard (1991). FAB: A Useful Tool for the Job-seeking Marketing Students, *Marketing Education Review*, Winter 1991, Vol. 1 Issue 2, p 60.

Solomon, Michael R. (1983). The Role of Products as Social Stimuli: A Symbolic Interactionism Perspective, *Journal of Consumer Research* 10: pp. 319–329.

Vinson, Donald E.; Scott Jerome E.; Lamont, Lawrence M. (1977). The Role of Personal Values in Marketing and Consumer Behavior, *Journal of Marketing*, pp. 44–50.

Wansink, Brian (2003). Using laddering to understand and leverage a brand's equity, *Qualitative Market Research: An International Journal*, Vol. 6 Issue 2, p. 111.

Young, Shirley; Feigin, Barbara (1975). Using the Benefit Chain for Improved Strategy Formulation, *Journal of Marketing*, Vol. 3 Issue 3, pp. 72–74.

Zeithaml, V.A. (1988). Consumer Perceptions of Price, Quality, and Value: A Means End Model and Synthesis of Evidence, *Journal of Marketing*, Vol. 52, pp. 2–22.

Books

Aaker, A. David (1996). *Building Strong Brands,* The Free Press.

Arnould, Eric J.; Price, Linda L.; Zinkhan, George M. (2004). *Consumers*, 2nd edition, McGraw-Hill/Irwin.

Balsley, Ronald D.; Birsner, Patricia E. (1987). *Selling: Marketing Personified*, The Dryden Press, Chicago.

Futrell, Charles M. (1984). *Fundamentals of Selling*, Homewood, IL:Irwin.

Futrell, Charles M. (2006). *Fundamentals of Selling*, 9th edition, Homewood, McGraw-Hill/Irwin.

Gustafsson, Conny; Rennemark, Rune (2002). *Säljande reklam.* Liber AB, Malmö.

Ilmonen, Kaj (2007). *Johan on markkinat – kulutuksen sosiologista tarkastelua,* Vastapaino, Tampere.

Kahle, Lynn R. (1983). *Social Values and Social Change: Adaption to Life in America,* Praeger Publishers, New York.

Karrus, Kaij E. (2005). *Logistiikka,* Werner Söderström Osakeyhtiö.

Kotler, Philip (2003). *Marketing Management,* 11th edition, Prentice Hall International Editions.

Keller, Kevin Lane (2003). *Strategic Brand Management: Building, Measuring, and Managing Brand Equity,* 2nd edition, Prentice Hall.

Maslow, Abraham H. (1970). *Motivation and Personality,* 2nd edition, Harper & Row, Publishers.

Peter, Paul J.; Olson Jerry C. (1996). *Consumer Behaviour and Marketing Strategy,* 4th Edition, Irwin.

Peter, Paul J.; Olson Jerry C.; Grunert, Klaus G. (1999). *Consumer Behaviour and Marketing Strategy,* European Edition, McGraw-Hill.

Rokeach, Milton (1973). *The Nature of Human Values,* The Free Press, New York.

Rokeach, Milton (1979). *Understanding Human Values, Individual and Societal,* The Free Press, New York.

Theses

Baker, Susan (1996). *Extending Means-End Theory Through an Investigation of the Consumer Benefit/Price Sensitivity Relationship in Two Markets,* a PhD dissertation at the Cranfield University.

Henriksson, Robert (2005). *Identifiering av kundupplevd nytta: En studie om upplevd nytta med Kickbike sparkcykeln,* a Master's thesis at Swedish School of Economics and Business Administration.

Dictionaries

AMA (American Marketing Association) http://www.marketingpower.com/live/mg-dictionary.php, (information retrieved on 30.5.2005).

Bonniers stora lexikon (1987). Bonnier Fakta Bokförlag, Stockholm.

Bonniers svenska ordbok (1991). Bonnier Fakta Bokförlag, Stockholm.

Bonniers synonymordbok, Walter, Göran (2000). Albert Bonniers Förlag, Stockholm.

Chambers English Dictionary, 7th edition (1988). W & R Chambers Ltd, and Cambridge University Press.

Dictionary of Marketing Terms (1981). Shapiro, Irving J., Fourth Edition, Littlefield, Adams & Company, Totowa, N.J.

MAANZ (The Marketing Association of Australia & New Zealand) http://www.marketing.org.au/glossaries.aspx, (Information retrieved on 30.5.2005).

Nationalencyklopedin (1994). Bokförlaget Bra Böcker, Höganäs.

Norstedts svenska ordbok (1991). Språkdata, Sture Allén och Nordstedts Förlag AB.

Nykysuomen sanakirja (1961). Kolmas painos, Suomalaisen Kirjallisuuden Seura, Werner Söderström Osakeyhtiö.

Oxford Textbook of Marketing (2000). Blois, Keith; Dibb, Sally; Oxford University Press/Books, p. 380, 34p.

Svensk ordbok (1986). Språkdata och Esselte Studium AB.

Verbal sources

Futrell, M. Charles, markkinoinnin professori, Lowry Mays College & Graduate School of Business at Texas A&M University, e-mail 18.3.2005

Companies

Kickbike Worldwide Oy, www.kickbike.com

* * *